Raised-bed Gardening

How to Grow More in Less Space

Tom Sardarov

Table of Contents

Introduction

Starting a new garden? Looking to up your gardening game this year? Try growing in raised beds! They're available in a variety of materials, dimensions, and heights — including waist-high, no-bend elevated gardens — so there's sure to be one right for you.

Here are some of the many benefits to growing in raised beds vs. in-ground beds:

The soil warms up and dries out faster in spring, so you can start planting earlier.

You can fill beds with the optimal soil for the plants you're growing. (This is especially important if your soil is heavy clay or very sandy.) Use a mix of topsoil and compost to start plants off right.

They're more productive. Plants grow faster and produce more.

They can be used to define a space, helping to keep pets and kids out of the garden.

Soil stays loose and fluffy because you won't be compacting it by walking in the beds.

Problems with rabbits and woodchucks nibbling your veggies? Elevated raised beds keep plants out of their reach — and make it easier for you to reach plants without bending or kneeling.

They're available in a variety of materials, so you'll find beds to complement your home and landscape style.

They're easier to cover, so you can protect plants from insects and other pests, as well as chilly and/or windy weather.

Chapter 1
MAKING RAISED BEDS
WORK FOR YOU

Practical considerations

Lifting materials to a raised height can be hard work and if done incorrectly can cause strain or even injury. For example, using a watering can is much easier when watering crops at a lower height, whereas lifting a full can up to raised bed height can be awkward. Of course, there are solutions to this, such as using irrigation systems or a hose and breakers. Lifting other heavy materials such as wheelbarrow loads of compost or heavy plants in pots can also be harder. However, you can use low ramps or scaffold boards to push small amounts of compost in on wheelbarrows. Alternatively, just use smaller, lighter containers such as buckets to lift materials.

How high is too high?

In raised beds, tall climbing plants such as French and runner beans or hops might actually end up being too tall for you to reach if you grow them up teepees and upright structures, meaning you then need to use ladders to harvest and tie in your crops. However, there are dwarf versions of these plants that are just as easy to grow and will make harvesting and maintenance very easy.

Budget

Construction costs for raised beds are much higher than when growing crops directly in the soil. Whether using bricks, rocks, or lumber, materials usually have to be bought. This is in addition to nails, screws, and the tools to put them together such as drills, jigsaws, and hammers. Then there are the costs of the planting material. In an ideal world, people would have a pile of home-made compost that could be used to fill the beds, but the reality is that most people will have to import material into the garden. However, the initial outlay is well worth it, because in the long term, the beds will last for a good few years and will increase efficiency, with larger harvests for vegetable crops. In addition, raised beds should reduce the need for anti-slug and -snail measures, because the beds raise the produce further off the ground.

Retain moisture

Depending on what type of raised bed you choose, it could result in having to water the plants more regularly than ones grown in the ground during the growing period. This is because raised beds provide better drainage. However, solutions such as hugelkultur and keyhole gardening provide improvements to the soil structure that help to retain moisture rather than losing it.

Allow adequate space

Constructing raised beds will reduce the amount of growing space you have outdoors. This is because you will need space to move between them. Ideally, the space should be at least wide enough to get a wheelbarrow between the beds, so this can result in losing invaluable planting areas to paths. The benefit, though, is that the raised bed will increase efficiency overall, and you can plant closer together due to the extra depth in your raised bed and the improved drainage. Reducing the amount of growing space could be an advantage if you are looking to simplify your garden or reduce the maintenance, or create some sort of structure to its layout.

To DIY or not to DIY?

There is nothing complicated about making a raised bed. Armed with a few basic tools, construction of a bed is very easy. Of course, you can employ a landscape gardener to construct them for you, or buy pre-built kits that you assemble yourself, but this will incur further costs.

Weeding and harvesting

Hand weeding is much easier at a raised height, but using a hoe can be tricky due to the angle, as can digging out deep perennial weeds with a fork. Crops that require digging up with a spade, such as Jerusalem artichokes and potatoes, can also be more awkward in raised beds. It is always best to avoid walking on the raised beds, so if you think you will need to dig over the soil then do consider the size and shape of the raised bed before you build it. Think carefully about which crops are practical to grow. Crops that require digging can instead be grown in compost bags, where the bags can be ripped open to harvest instead. Ideally, you want to work to measurements that allow you to reach all areas of the bed to weed or harvest efficiently. You can always use a hand fork, trowel, or hand hoe for digging, which can comfortably be done from the side of the raised bed.

RAISED BED BUILDING MATERIALS

Once we decide to build a raised bed, the next step is to decide what material to

use.

Considerations for Raised Bed Building Materials

Functional and/or Visually Appealing

Cost of Materials

Life Span of Material

Hold soil only and/or provide place to sit or walk

Organic Requirements

Does the material leach chemicals or change the pH?

Functional and/or Visually Appealing - I think my simple wooden and stacked

stone raised beds look nice, but the beds are primarily built to be inexpensive

and functional. The planting areas are confined by the frames or stones and the

pathways are lined with landscape fabric and crushed stone to keep unwanted

weeds and grass out and to provide wide walkways that are clean, relatively

level and dry.

We have all seen amazing stone landscaping and raised beds designed not only to look very nice, but also to be functional and that will last for many years.

Cost of Materials - Few of us grow tomatoes at home to save money. We can

not compete with the ag-industry for price per pound. We do it because the agindustry

can not provide the same fresh home-grown taste and quality. I joke

with friends and family about spending hundreds of dollars per pound just to

have home-grown tomatoes, but that is a huge exaggeration. Truth is, it makes

more sense to me to spend a little money, time and effort on something I can eat

instead of mowing grass.

If time, space and money were no object, most of us would have skilled stone

masons build beautiful stone "seat-walled" raised beds. But most of us are not

likely to spend thousands of dollars for a stone raised bed when an untreated

lumber raised bed can be built for less than $50.

If we think of the cost of building raised beds in terms of the square foot cost of

building a wall, the square foot cost of common building materials shows that untreated dimensional lumber is least expensive. The cost to build a

wall with concrete block is almost twice as much. Railroad ties cost more than

concrete block, especially if the seven inch side is used as the wall instead of the nine inch side. The cost of pressure treated lumber is twice as much as untreated lumber.

Garden block is a nice looking option, but cost about three times as much as untreated lumber .

Life Span of Material - Untreated wood will probably last 10 years in my cold dry climate, but may not last but a few years in warm and wet climates like found in the Southern U.S. Pressure Treated Wood is supposed to last for 20 years. Used railroad ties have already been discarded but will last for many moreyears. Concrete blocks should last for a long time, but some are brittle and will easily break if they are not filled with soil or mortared in place. I have also seen some landscape or garden blocks that have totally deteriorated from freezing and thawing in about 10 years.

Hold soil only and/or provide place to sit or walk - A new trend in landscaping is the Seat Wall. Why not build a raised bed that looks and sits like a seat wall? A typical 2x12 board does a good job of holding soil inside the raised bed, but on edge, a single board makes a poor seat. Additional lumber could be attached to the tops of the raised bed to create a better seat. Most true seat walls are made of stone, concrete or garden blocks.

Organic Requirements - Many people that start raised bed gardening do so with the idea of growing some of their own food that has little or no pesticides.

If the garden is sprayed, they know what kind, how much spray was used and when it was last used. They may or may not buy into the whole "Organic" idea.

I am not going to get into all the details here, but I know it is possible to have Arsenic treated wood in contact with soil, food or animals and still be Certified Organic by the Federal Government. I like the idea of knowing where my food comes from and that it has not been poisoned and does not have additives I don't want. But since the Federal Government is in charge of the Organic Program, it works like everything else the Federal Government touches. I am not convinced we are getting what we pay for or have been led to believe.

If you are interested in following the Organic Program, you need to be aware that some building materials that could be used for raised beds may leach chemicals into the soil or water.

Does the Material Leach chemicals or affect soil pH? - Read my take on using pressure treated wood in the garden here:

The pressure treated wood available at most building supply stores will leach copper into the soil. Copper is not a big deal in soil and not a big problem to people, but it is a big problem in aquatic systems.

Wood treated with Arsenic is still available for agricultural purposes leaches arsenic into the soil.

Soil in contact with concrete will have elevated pH because of the lime in the concrete. This is good for some plants, but is not good for plants that prefer low pH.

Metal materials can leach metals into the soil especially at pH 5.5 or lower - fortunately, most plants prefer pH above 5.5.

Raised Bed Building Materials

I have seen a variety of materials used to create raised beds. The following list includes those materials.

Lumber - treated or untreated - some untreated wood like cedar and redwood are naturally rot resistant

Landscape timbers Railroad ties (creosote)

Rock or Stone; mortared or loose stacked Concrete blocks; mortared or stacked Bricks; mortared or stacked

Formed concrete Corrugated metal and culverts Corrugated fiberglass Old tires Other Repurposed Materials.

HOW DEEP?

The depth required for your raised bed will depend on various factors: the type of
plants you are intending to grow, and whether the bed is on a patio, has a bottom
to it, or sits directly on the soil below. If the bed is directly on soil, then plants with
larger roots will eventually grow through the depth of the raised bed and into the
ground beneath, meaning that the height of the raised bed is less important.

Salad crops, annuals, and herbs

If you are planning on growing only a few salad crops each year, then about 4 inches is sufficient depth. Salad crops are very shallow rooting and will even produce decent leafy crops in a window box, so a deep raised bed is not essential. You may, of course, have other reasons for growing them in a higher raised bed, such as ease of maintenance, or for the sake of appearance. Annual bedding plants such as busy lizzie, petunia, lobelia, begonia, annual rudbeckia, and cosmos have similar requirements and won't produce large root systems, meaning they will thrive in shallow soil. Many perennial herbs, such as rosemary, mint, and thyme, originate from the Mediterranean region, where they happily grow in arid and rocky soil conditions, so they won't require a deep root run either.

Herbaceous perennials, deeper-rooted vegetables, and ornamental grasses

Herbaceous plants will have a much larger root system than annuals and therefore require a deeper raised bed. Vegetables such as carrots, potatoes, cabbages, peas, beans, and so on will also need a deeper root run. For most, a depth of at least 12 inches is needed to allow them to grow to their full potential. They will grow in more shallow conditions, but it may be necessary to feed and water them more to compensate for the lack of soil or compost.

Shrubs and fruit bushes

Most fruit bushes and shrubs will require at least 20 inches depth of soil to allow them to fully develop and grow. It is possible for them to grow in shallower conditions but their growth will be stunted considerably and they probably won't live as long as if they were planted in deeper soil.

Trees

As a rule of thumb, what you see above the ground is usually mirrored by the root system below the ground, so you can imagine the root system required for a large tree. Of course, trees are very adaptable, and you only have to look at bonsai trees to see how their growth can be curtailed to suit the available space. Some trees can be bought on dwarf rootstock, which reduces their overall size. However, ideally trees should be given at least 3-4 feet of depth in a raised bed.

SITING YOUR RAISED BED

The key to successful gardening is matching the right plants with the position of
the raised bed. In small gardens, you may not have much choice as to where the
beds are constructed, but thankfully there are plants to suit every aspect, whether
it be a shady, damp corner or a dry, sun-baked bed.

Shady corners

If possible and space allows, it is best to select an open, sunny site. The majority of plants require maximum sunlight to thrive. With more of their leaves exposed to the sunlight, they produce more sugars, which sweetens the taste of any fruit or vegetables that they produce. However, if your garden is in the shade for most of the day, don't despair. Some plants are shade-loving: for example, leafy crops such as cabbages, spinach, and summer salads prefer it slightly cooler. The beds will also have less tendency to dry out from the sun and the cool root system will mean that vegetable plants are far less likely to bolt. There are also plenty of ornamental plants that thrive in shady corners, such as hostas, ferns, epimediums, and hellebores.

Check the light

Before building a raised bed it is a good idea to examine where the sunlight falls in the garden to maximize the sunlight. It may sound obvious, but do bear in mind, particularly in small gardens, that a flower bed that is in the sunlight on the ground might be moved slightly out of the light once it is raised. Tree canopies, walls, and roofs might suddenly block an area that is usually bathed in sunlight when directly on the ground.

Understanding the aspect

The sun rises in the east and sets in the west. In the middle of the day the sun is in the south. For this reason, southfacing raised beds will be much warmer and sunnier than those constructed on the north side of the house. Ideally, a raised bed should be in sunlight for as much of the day as possible. So if your back yard faces north, but you are lucky enough to have a spacious front yard, then consider constructing your raised bed there. Also, remember that the sun is much higher in summer than in winter, so if you are hoping to extend the season, do check to see whether your garden still receives sunlight when at its lowest height.

Creating more light

Another method of allowing more sunlight into your garden is to cut back overhanging and overgrown vegetation and branches. Consider asking your neighbors if they are happy to reduce the height of their boundaries or cut back some of the trees in their garden if it is affecting the light in your garden. Lowering your boundary fence could also allow more light in, although, of course, this could be at the cost of your privacy.

Location, location, location

You should also give practical issues consideration when deciding where to site your raised bed. If you are planning on growing vegetables or herbs, then you may wish to place it near the kitchen window or back door to make it as easy as possible to grab fresh produce when cooking. Perhaps you wish to create more privacy from your neighbors— raising the height of your garden on the boundaries by placing raised beds there will help with this. They can also be placed around a patio or seating area to create a sense of privacy. If you are planning to grow tall plants in your raised bed, it's best not to site it near to the house as it could end up blocking your view of the garden.

Providing shelter

Like human beings, plants often prefer some protection from the elements. Exposure to the wind can decimate the leaves on plants. Furthermore, it can cause plants to quickly dry out as it sucks away any moisture in the soil. Strong winds during blossoming season will cause low yields in fruit trees and bushes, as pollinating insects are unable to fly in windy weather. One of the solutions is to choose tough, tenacious plants that will tolerate the wind. Most plants that thrive in coastal locations are suitable. However, if you wish to grow tender plants or even most types of vegetables, some protection from the wind is required. Most small gardens, particularly in towns, will already have adequate shelter from winds as they will be surrounded by hedges, walls, and fences. In larger gardens it is best to avoid creating raised beds in exposed conditions such as on top of a hill. The best type of windbreak is a hedge, since it slows down the excessive blasts of wind, but is semipermeable, meaning that there is still some air circulation. This is important as it helps to prevent the build-up of pests and diseases, particularly fungus, which thrive in stagnant, still conditions. Non-permeable structures such as walls and fences will prevent some wind damage, but they can also have a detrimental effect, as sometimes the wind can buffer along the top edge and drop down onto the raised bed with extra strength.

Frost pockets

Many plants will suffer if you place your raised bed in a frost pocket. Frost generally collects in the lowest part of the garden, as the cold air drifts into it, replacing any warmer air that rises. The effect is often exacerbated if the cold air is prevented from circulating by a permanent structure, such as a wall or fence at the lowest end of the garden. Young seedlings will quickly get zapped by the cold weather, while young, tender shoots or blossoms will shrivel up and die. It will reduce the length of the available growing season too, as the soil will be too cold to sow anything until late spring, and plants will quickly die back in fall. Avoiding cold, frosty sites will allow early spring sowings and extend the season well into the following late autumn. If it is not possible to avoid a frost pocket, then be prepared to cover plants and sow later in the season to avoid the disappointment of losing your plants to a harsh frost.

Chapter 2

PLAN YOUR GARDEN

Size

Your garden will be laid out in square or rectangular boxes separated by walking aisles. Build your boxes from materials like wood, bricks, or blocks. If y o u don't like the idea of common wood, which will eventually rot or be eaten by termites, use a more expensive wood like cedar or redwood. You can even use some of the manmade composite "wood" or recycled plastic or vinyl. T h e wood I like best is free wood. You can usually get it from any construction site, but always ask the foreman first.

If y ou decide to use lumber, you'll be happy to know the advantage of 4 x 4 gardens is that all lumber comes in 8-foot lengths. Most home improvement centers will cut it in half for you at little or **10** cost. Your boxes can be made from just about any material except treated wood because the chemicals used to treat the wood are not something you want leaching into your garden.

How Much Is Enough?

If you're figuring a S FG for an adult, remember that:

1. One 4 x 4 Square Foot Garden box (equal to 16 square feet) will supply enough produce to make a salad for one person every day of the growing season.

2. One more 4 x 4 box will supply the daily supper vegetables for that person.

3. Just one more 4 x 4 box will supply that person with extra of everything for preserving, special crops, showing off, or giving away.

So, each adult needs one, two, or three large boxes of 4 x 4 , depending on how much they want. In square feet, that i s 1 6 , 3 2 , or 48 square feet.

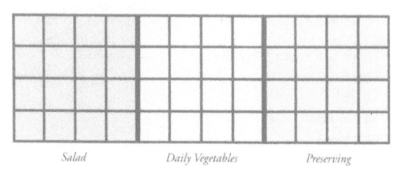

Salad   Daily Vegetables   Preserving

If you're figuring a SFG for a child, remember that:

1. One 3 x 3 Square Foot Garden box (equal to 9 square feet) will supply enough produce to make a salad for one child every day of the growing season.

2. One more 3 x 3 box will supply supper vegetables for that child every day.

3. Just one more 3 x 3 box will supply the child with extra of everything for show-and-tell or science projects at school, special crops, showing off, or giving away. So, each child needs one, two, or three small boxes of 3 x 3 , depending on how much they will eat. In square feet, that's 9, 1 8 , or 27 square feet.

Suggestion: Since the kids will grow into teenagers, you may just want to make everyone's box a 4 x 4 . On the other hand, different sizes make the garden look interesting and more personable. The 3 x 3 can later on be stacked on top of a 4 x 4 to start a pyramid garden—but more about designing your garden later.

BASIC CONSTRUCTION OF A WOODEN RAISED BED

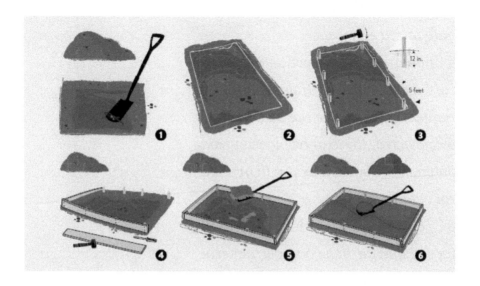

1 | *If the soil where the raised bed is to be constructed is of good quality, then this should be removed and saved for later to top off the bed.*

2 | *Use string to mark out the perimeter of the bed.*

3 | *Raised beds will require retaining stakes that are 2 inches by 2 inches wide that should be banged into the corners using a sledge hammer. The sides will also require support, with stakes placed every 5 feet. Drive these approximately 12 inches into*

the ground.

4 | Next, attach the retaining wooden boards to the stakes using galvanized screws.

5 | Fill up the lower section of the raised bed with soil. If you had to remove grass where the bed was to be constructed, this can be placed upside down in the bottom as it will gradually rot over the season.

6 | Top off the bed with a 50:50 mix of topsoil and garden compost/general purpose compost.

BASIC CONSTRUCTION OF A BRICK RAISED BED

Brick raised beds are harder to build than wooden ones, requiring slightly more practical skills, such as bricklaying, but nothing too diffi cult to learn. They should last a lifetime once constructed and provide a strong, sturdy bed that looks great in most locations, whether it be a garden or a front or back yard.

1 | Use string to mark out the perimeter of the bed.

2 | Construct a concrete footing. This will prevent the bed from sinking. Dig out a trench 20 inches deep and the width of two bricks.

Line the bottom with a concrete foundation (one part cement, two and a half parts sand, three and a half parts gravel) to a depth of 6 inches. Leave to dry.

3 | Mix up your cement, using three parts sand to one part cement. Water should be added to make it an easy-to-use consistency that isn't too sloppy but is flexible enough to spread onto the brickwork. Adding plasticizer will help keep the cement flexible.

4 | Start to lay the courses of bricks, two bricks wide. Bed each brick onto a 1 inch layer of cement. Start the second layer with half a brick so that the bricks are staggered with the courses below it, as this will make it stronger. Use strings and a level to ensure that each course is level.

5 | The first three layers will take you up to ground level. Continue above ground level until you reach your desired height.

6 | Pairs of chamfered coping bricks should be cemented all around the top edge for protection from dampness and to make it look more attractive.

7 | Line the inside of the walls with a permeable membrane.

PATHS

If you are planning on having more than one raised bed, you need to think carefully about the paths that will lead around and between them. Paths form the backbone and structure to any garden design and are essential in ensuring that the key elements of the garden can be reached. They need to be functional and practical, but ideally should also look good and fit in with the style of your raised bed. For example, a formal brick raised bed may look incongruous with a rustic woodchip path around it.

THE ANSWER LIES IN THE SOIL

Having the right soil conditions is essential if you want your plants to perform at their best. Some plants have very specific requirements in terms of the level of acidity or alkalinity that they will thrive in, though most garden plants prefer neutral conditions and will tolerate slightly acidic or alkaline variations. It is worth checking the pH level of your soil first in case it is extremely acidic or alkaline.

ACIDIC-SOIL-LOVING
PLANTS INCLUDE...

HOLLIES
PRIMULAS
RHODODENDRONS
AZALEAS
MAPLES
MAGNOLIAS
CAMELLIAS
BLUEBERRIES
CRANBERRIES

ALKALINE-SOIL-LOVING
PLANTS INCLUDE...

CEANOTHUS
LAVENDER
CLEMATIS
DIANTHUS
GERANIUM
CAMPANULA
LIGUSTRUM
BUDDLEJA
CHOISYA

GETTING READY FOR PLANTING

It's all in the preparation! Whether your plants thrive or struggle in their raised bed is largely down to how well you prepare the soil before planting. Planting a raised bed is very similar to planting a flower border or vegetable patch when growing in normal conditions. However, plants are occasionally planted closer together in a raised bed, particularly in deep beds, as it is assumed roots will go further downwards.

Groundwork

The soil or compost should be prepared thoroughly before beginning to plant. All plants have different requirements for growing—such as spacing between plants, sunlight and moisture, and soil type—and some are more particular than others. There is usually information on the packet of seeds or plant label which you can check if you're unsure.

If plants have been grown in the soil before, dig it over and remove any perennial weeds. It is usually best not to walk on raised beds to avoid compacting the soil, but depending on the height and width of the bed, it may be possible to lay planks or scaffold boards across the bed in order to access the soil, assuming the raised bed is strong enough to take the weight. If vegetables are to be planted, then the soil will benefit from having well-rotted manure or garden compost added. Dig this in, rake the soil level, and allow it to settle for a few days.

Filling up

Don't overfill your beds. Although the soil level will gradually drop slightly, if beds are filled above the edge of the bed, then soil and water will spill out. Aim to have the level of the soil about 1-3 inches below the top of the bed. The levels can always be topped off with mulch or compost later in the year. In fact, you'll probably want to add mulch or compost each year to improve the soil, so leaving a gap for this is a good idea.

If climbing structures are required for plants such as runner beans, climbing roses, or clematis, then it is best to get these in place first to avoid trampling over the plants at a later date. Climbing structures can include teepees, trellises, or archways.

Planting out

Before planting anything into the raised bed it is best to give the plants a good watering first. Sit the plants in trays, water the soil until saturated, and then leave them in the trays to soak up any more water if needed for about an hour. Prepare a planting hole in the bed prior to removing each plant from its pot to reduce the time the root ball is exposed to daylight and thereby minimize its chances of drying out. Once the planting hole is dug, the plant should be eased out of its pot. If the plant is rootbound, the roots should be teased out to prevent them from continuing to spiral around once planted, as this will eventually strangle the plant. This is more important with trees and shrubs as they have a longer life expectancy than herbaceous plants and will therefore be more affected.

Most trees and shrubs should not be planted any deeper in the ground than they were in the pot. It's also important to ensure that the plants are at the correct planting distance from each other. If you are unsure, then check the plant label. The key is that once the plants have grown to their correct height a minimal amount of soil is left exposed. This is because bare soil will enable weeds to germinate and the rain and wind will cause any nutrients to leach out.

WATERING

Plants grown in raised beds will require more watering than plants grown directly in the ground due to the extra drainage the raised beds provide. The extra warmth of a raised bed and exposure to wind will also cause the soil to dry out faster. In summer it is particularly important that plants are kept well watered, otherwise they will rapidly start wilting and possibly even die. In fact, lack of water is the number one reason for plants dying in the garden. However, there are a few methods of reducing the amount of water that the plants will need.

Mulch

Try to avoid leaving soil exposed in the raised bed as

moisture will quickly evaporate. Instead, cover it over with mulch such as garden manure. Digging organic matter into the soil will also help retain moisture.

Choose drought-tolerant plants

Choose plants that will cope with dry conditions. Many ornamental plants, including grasses, bamboos, and modernstyle

North American prairie plants, will tolerate dry conditions. Herbs are also fairly drought tolerant.

Irrigation

Consider using irrigation in the garden but avoid sprinklers, as these throw a lot of water in the air and very often don't hit the target. Instead, use soaker hoses which lie on the surface of the raised bed in among the plants and gently trickle out water around the root system. They can be placed on timers so they only produce water for short amounts of time. A home-made soaker hose can easily be made by puncturing an old hose with tiny holes using a fork.

Timing

Avoid watering plants in the middle of the day. This can result in the water evaporating before it has had a chance to percolate down into the roots. It can also cause leaf scorch if wet leaves get caught by the midday sun. Watering is most effective in the evening (although the prolonged dampness during the evening can encourage slugs) or in the morning.

Accuracy

If possible, avoid watering with a hose as water can be lost due to excess splashing. Very often it doesn't accurately target the root system, instead splashing over the leaves, flowers, and surrounding areas. If feasible, use a watering can and specifically target the area around the roots.

Water sumps

Build up small mounds of soil in a ring around a plant to create a sort of bowl that you can then fill with water. This holds the water in place around the roots, ensuring that it doesn't drain off away from the plant.

COMPOSTING

Every good garden needs a good composting system, and it doesn't need to be complicated or high tech either. Not only is it free, you don't have to drive to the garden center to transport it in bulky bags and your home-made compost will probably be better and more natural than any product you can buy. Composting is a fantastic way of recycling kitchen and garden waste, and the resulting healthy, nutrient-rich compost can be added to the soil in your raised beds. There are lots of different types of composting systems available, including keyhole and hugelkultur (see pages 72–79), which rely on the natural decomposition of plant material to feed the raised bed. Compost bins can either be incorporated as part of the raised bed, or can be in a separate area of the garden.

How many bins?

If space allows, three compost heaps are ideal in a garden (though two is workable): one for adding waste to, one which is in the process of being left to rot, and a third which is already rotted and is to be used on the raised beds.

Keep the compost covered to prevent the material washing and leaching away. However, check on the heap to ensure it isn't drying out. If it is, then add water to the heap.

Turning the heap

Ideally, compost heaps should be turned monthly with a fork to enable air to get into the material, which will speed up the process of decomposition. However, it is not essential— you could turn it once a year, it will just take longer for the material to decompose. If possible, place an empty compost bay next to the heap, so that it can be turned into the empty bay and left.

Types of compost bins

Drum

The most common type of compost bin is the large plastic drum type, with an access hatch at the bottom and a lid.

Tumblers

Some compost bins have a rotating drum which saves you having to turn over the compost material with a fork.

Recycled containers

Any container can be used to hold compost. Some gardeners use woven bulk bags, while others use stacks of rubber tires, adding additional tires onto the stack as more compost is produced.

Troubleshooting

Getting a good quality compost is all about getting the right balance between the two main ingredients, carbon and nitrogen. Ideally, the balance should be two parts carbon to one part nitrogen. Carbon is supplied by material such as newspaper, dry leaves, wood chips, and bark. Nitrogen comes from green material such as grass clippings or green garden waste such as herbaceous plant material. If the compost is smelly and slimy then there is probably too much nitrogen in it and more carbon material should be added and mixed in. If the compost is too dry and not rotting then there is too much carbon and more green waste should be added. Water from the rain barrel can also be added.

An ideal mix for the majority of plants to grow in a raised bed is 50 percent topsoil and 50 percent garden compost, although more specialized plants such as alpines or acidicsoil-loving plants will have different requirements.

The compost is ready when it has rotted down into a dark brown, crumbly material and has a pleasant earthy, woodland aroma. It shouldn't smell unpleasant or feel excessively moist and slimy.

Liquid lunch

There are various fertilizers that can be added to your raised bed to boost the plants' health, speed of growth, and production of flowers and fruit. The simplest natural fertilizer, though, can be made easily from plants in the garden, particularly comfrey or nettles.

: Harvest comfrey or nettle leaves and place them into a bucket of water. Place a brick onto the leaves to hold them under the water.

: Leave them to "brew" for a few weeks—be warned, they do smell unpleasant when they're starting to break down.

: Filter the liquid through a sieve to remove any unrotted leaves. Use a funnel to decant the liquid into plastic milk cartons or bottles to store.

: Dilute this comfrey or nettle concentrate in a watering can at a ratio of ten parts water to one part liquid feed when using to feed the plants. Use once or twice every two weeks to give your herbaceous plants and vegetables a nitrogenrich boost during the growing season.

To dig or not to dig

Once you have filled your raised beds with compost and soil they won't need digging again for the first year. However, in the second year, you will need to consider whether to dig over the beds thoroughly or leave them "undug."
In the world of gardening, opinions are divided.
Traditionalists believe that the soil should be dug
over before planting, the theory being that it breaks
up any compaction and clods of earth, exposes pests
to the cold weather and to predators such as birds and
hedgehogs, removes the roots of weeds, and encourages

deeper rooting of plants. However, there is a school of thought that believes digging over the ground damages soil structure, disturbs beneficial bugs in the soil, and encourages weed seed to germinate. Instead, they advocate adding layers of organic matter and mulch over the existing soil, allowing the rain or worms to take it down into the soil.

PESTS AND DISEASES

Unfortunately, there are many pests and diseases that can strike the plants in your
raised bed at any time. One of the best methods of combating pests and diseases is
to ensure that your plants are as strong, healthy, and resilient as possible. The other
is to know the warning signs that pests or diseases are at work, and to react quickly.

Pests

Here are some of the more common pests that can be found in the garden. If you are working hard to grow delicious fruit or vegetables, it will be worth taking a few preventative measures to ensure that it is you who dines on them and not any of these creatures. Chemical controls can, of course, be used and are readily available from garden centers. However, there are nonchemical methods that are also worth trying, which will have a less detrimental side effect on the environment.

Slugs

Slugs happily munch through young plants and seedlings, and disappointed gardeners can find their entire vegetable crop devoured in just a few nights if left unmanaged. One of the benefits of growing vegetables in raised beds is that the plants are further off the ground and out of the reach of slugs and snails. The elevation will mean fewer of these pests, but it won't

stop them entirely. It will also mean they are out of the reach of

hedgehogs, one of the main natural predators of slugs, though the raised height will make the slugs more accessible to birds. Slugs that do make it into your raised bed will tend to cluster around the sides and edges, so by keeping a

regular vigilant watch you should be able easily to

pick them off and dispose of them in whichever way

you see fit. Another method is to make a beer trap.

This involves sinking a container into the ground

so that the top of the container is level with the soil,

and filling it with beer. The theory is that the slug

drinks the beer and then cannot get out and drowns.

If you don't like the idea of wasting beer, then any

other sugary solution should be enticing enough to

capture them. Alternatively, you can scatter orange

and grapefruit peels around the garden to attract the slugs, making them much easier to gather up in the evening.

Slugs prefer moist conditions, so water your plants early in the morning rather than the evening, when slugs begin to emerge.

Grit, eggshells, and other coarse materials can be scattered around a plant to prevent slugs and snails from crossing over to feast on them. Copper barrier tape can be bought from garden centers to place around plants. The material gives a slight electric shock to these pests to keep them at bay. They also try to avoid salt as it dehydrates them, leading to an unpleasant death. Seaweed can be used to create a barrier due to its salty content.

By far the most effective option, however, is slug pellets. Aluminium sulphate pellets are thought to be more environmentally friendly. Use them sparingly, to reduce the likelihood of them causing harm to animals. Just a few pellets around each plant should be sufficient. Seedlings and newly planted plants are the most vulnerable, and it is only these that will really need protection.

Birds

Birds can be beneficial in the garden and can help keep levels of small grubs and aphids down to a manageable level. However, the reality is that they will also enjoy munching on your crops—not so much of a problem, of course, if you're only growing ornamentals. Pigeons are particularly fond of brassicas such as cabbages, kale, and sprouts, while bullfinches will peck out the ripening buds on fruit trees. And most birds will help themselves to any ripening fruit. The best way to keep your crops safe from birds is to cover them with a bird net. Thankfully, growing crops in raised beds makes it easier to cover them as there is already a base to the structure. A basic protective fruit cage can simply be made by lashing together bamboo canes to create a 6 foot structure above the raised bed. Remember to peg down the bottom of the net to prevent birds from sneaking in underneath. A specifically designed bird-scaring humming line can also be used as a deterrent over a raised bed. It should be tied tightly between two posts, which will cause it to hum in the wind, deterring the birds from visiting your crops.

Aphids

Aphids are a common pest found on plants, often on new shoots and leaves. They can be removed simply by washing them off with soapy water. If caught early enough, they shouldn't have too much detrimental effect on the plants. An alternative method of controlling them is to buy ladybug or lacewing larvae and release them near the plants. The larvae feed on the aphids, quickly clearing up the problem for you. Some birds will also feed on aphids.

Cabbage white butterfly/caterpillar

These butterflies lay eggs on members of the cabbage family and the hatched caterpillars then feed on the leaves. Cover the plants with a fine mesh to prevent the adult insects landing on the plants.

Cabbage root fly

Larvae of the root fly feed on the roots of cabbages. You can buy specially made discs from garden centers to place around the base of the stem and prevent the root fly from landing and laying eggs.

Carrot fly

These flies are attracted by the scent of the carrot. Their tiny maggot offspring tunnel into the roots of both carrots and parsnips. To prevent attack, choose resistant varieties or cover them with a fine mesh to keep the tiny flies off your plants.

Japanese beetle

Japanese beetles will feed on the leaves of plants at any age. To control them you need to eliminate their larval form—the grubs. Visit your local garden center for *Bacillus thuringiensis* or Milky spore to apply to the lawn to eliminate the grubs.

Deer, woodchucks, and chipmunks

Deer, woodchucks, and chipmunks can all lay waste to a garden with astonishing efficiency. Sometimes they'll eat an entire plant to the ground, while other times they'll take a bite or two out of every single flower or fruit on the vine. Protect young trees by caging them with chicken wire. Sink the cage at least 12 inches into the ground, as woodchucks will burrow. Spray repellents on annuals, perennials, shrubs, vegetables, and small fruits to prevent deer, woodchucks, and chimpmunks from munching.

Mice and rats

Rodents love to feed on the seeds that you have just planted out, particularly peas and bean seeds. They will also feed on fruit, and they love sweetcorn. Traps can be placed to catch mice. There are poisons that can be used for rat infestations and advice can be sought from pest control companies.

Common diseases

There are many diseases that can affect the health of your plants. The trick is to try to catch the problem early to prevent it from spreading. Good plant hygiene and keeping your plant healthy are among the best methods of avoiding diseases, ensuring that they are strong enough to combat the problem if an attack should occur.

Powdery mildew

Gooseberry, squash, and blackcurrant plants are very susceptible to this fungus, which causes the leaves to be covered in a white powdery mildew. Keeping the plant healthy and watered at the roots should help the plant to combat an attack. Also, there are varieties that are resistance to this fungus.

Botrytis

This is a fungus that causes a grey mold to form on soft fruit and plants such as strawberries and lettuce. Eventually it leads to the plant rotting and dying back. It is commonly found in greenhouses and cold frames or areas with poor air circulation. Remove infected material and improve ventilation.

Canker

There are both bacterial and fungal cankers that can affect most fruit trees. In stone fruit such as plums and cherries it causes orange gum to ooze from infected branches and the trunk. On apple trees it causes sunken and withered areas on the branch. Where possible, infected material should be removed and saws and pruners should be sterilized.

Club root

This is a fungal infection that affects members of the cabbage family, causing the root system to swell and distort, eventually resulting in the plant dying back. There are varieties that have resistance. Increasing the pH can help as it tends to be worse in acidic soil. Crop rotation can also help to reduce the problem, by moving the cabbages into soil where the fungus isn't present.

Damping off

This is a common fungal problem found on seedlings that causes them to underdevelop and then rot.

It is usually found in the very early stages in a greenhouse. Remove infected material and improve the ventilation. Only water plants when the soil has just dried, as damp conditions cause the spread of this fungus.

Onion white rot

This fungus causes the browning and wilting of the foliage, eventually leading to the plant rotting and dying back. It affects onions, garlic, and leeks. The fungus can remain active in the ground for years, so replace the soil in a raised bed if the problem persists, or simply give in and grow a different crop.

Rust

There are a number of plants that can suffer from rust, which causes small orange pustules to appear on the leaves and stems. Infected material should be removed immediately to prevent it spreading.

Crop rotation should help to reduce the problem, as should increasing air circulation and ensuring the plants receive plenty of sunlight.

Blight

This mainly affects potatoes and tomatoes. (They are from the same family). It causes the leaves to turn brown and die back, resulting in the loss of the plant. Tomato plants should be disposed of as soon as it is spotted. If caught in time, the foliage of potato plants can be cut back, which might prevent the potatoes themselves from becoming infected.

Planting tomatoes in greenhouses can help to avoid the problem if you live in an area where it is a problem, as it gives them some protection from spores in the air.

CROP ROTATION

If you are planning on growing vegetables, it is worth considering having three or four individual raised beds or subdividing larger beds into sections. This will help you to manage your crops and enable them to be rotated each year.

Why rotate?

Crop rotation is a popular system among gardeners where specifi c groups of vegetables are grown in different beds each year. There are a variety of reasons for this, the main one being that it prevents a build-up of pests and diseases in the soil. Many are specifi c to a certain type of vegetable, so the theory is that by planting different types of crop in the soil each year it will prevent any problems from getting worse.

In addition, vegetables have different nutrient requirements, so growing them in different beds each year help to avoid a complete depletion of goodness in the soil. In fact, some vegetables will even gain nutrients by following another group of plants. For example, legumes (members of the pea family) fi x nitrogen in the soil, meaning that the vegetables planted in the soil the following season will benefi t from this extra boost of natural fertilizer.

Year 1
Roots and
potatoes—ideal
for breaking up soil
Year 3
Cabbages require rich
soil left by pea family
Year 2
Legumes and peas benefi t
from deep root run left by
root family

Do note that crop rotation is only for annual crops. Perennial fruit and vegetables such as rhubarb, strawberries, globe and Jerusalem artichokes, and asparagus are not included in the system. However, after a few years, they will also benefi t from being replanted in new beds so that they can take advantage of fresh soil and avoid pest and disease problems.

Most gardeners rotate crops over a three-year plan with the following categories:

: Root crops

: Legumes

: Brassicas

Note that brassicas and other leafy crops usually follow the legumes, which fi x the nitrogen that the brassicas use.

MAINTENANCE THROUGHOUT THE YEAR

There are a few essential jobs that you need to do throughout the year to ensure your raised beds are looking in tip-top form. Little and often is the best way to stay on top of the maintenance of the garden. Surprisingly, even in winter, when most plants are dormant and most of the vegetable beds lie empty, there are still plenty of garden tasks to take care of. Follow the seasonal guide on pages 62–63 to stay on top of gardening tasks throughout the year.

Staking plants

Many ornamental plants will require staking in early spring to prevent them flopping over the edges of the raised beds and onto the paths. The trick with staking to make it look natural is to get it in place before it is too late. It is best to allow the plant to grow through the staking structure rather than trying to get the plant upright once it has started to flop over. In the latter case it can look contrived, unnatural, and artificially trussed up. Staking materials include the following:

: Brush, such as from birch or willows, can be used to create an attractive rustic structure among the raised bed.

: Chain link stakes can be bought online or from a garden center. They are usually plastic or metal and link together to go around the plants.

: Single stakes are often used to support young trees and fruit bushes.

: Netting can be stretched tightly between posts to allow plants to scramble through them.

: Small sticks or twigs are ideal for allowing peas and some bean varieties to scramble through them.

: Willow teepees can be used to train up sweet peas or French and runner beans.

Chapter 3

HOW TO PLANT YOUR ALL NEW SQUARE FOOT GARDEN

VISUALIZE THE HARVEST

Begin by visualizing what you want to harvest. This simple step prevents you from planting too much. Picture a large plant like a head of cabbage. That single cabbage will take up a whole square foot so you can only plant one per square foot. It's the same with broccoli and cauliflower. Let's go to the opposite end of the spectrum and think of the small plants like radishes. Sixteen can fit into a single square foot. It's the same for onions and carrots—sixteen per square foot. (Yet that's a 3-inch spacing between plants, which is exactly the same spacing the seed packet recommends as it says "thin to 3 inches apart.")

Small, Medium, Large, Extra Large

Think of these plants as if they were shirt sizes. Shirts come in all four sizes: small, medium, large, and extra large, and so do our plants. It's that simple.

The extra large, of course, are those that take up the entire square foot—plants like cabbages, peppers, broccoli, cauliflower, and geraniums. Next are the large plants—those that can be planted four to a square foot, which equals 6 inches apart. Large plants include leaf lettuce, dwarf marigolds, Swiss chard, and parsley.

Several crops could be 1 per square foot if you let it grow to its full size or it can be planted 4 per square feet if you harvest the outer leaves throughout the season. This category includes parsley, basil, and even the larger heads of leaf lettuce and Swiss chard. Using the SFG method, you snip and constantly harvest the outer leaves of edible greens, so they don't take up as much space as in a conventional garden.

Medium plants come next. They fit nine to every square foot, which equals 4 inches apart. Medium plants include bush beans, beets, and large turnips.

PLANT SPACING

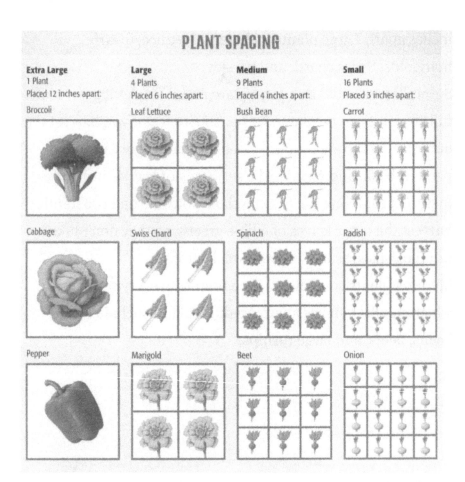

Extra Large
1 Plant
Placed 12 inches apart:
Broccoli

Cabbage

Pepper

Large
4 Plants
Placed 6 inches apart:
Leaf Lettuce

Swiss Chard

Marigold

Medium
9 Plants
Placed 4 inches apart:
Bush Bean

Spinach

Beet

Small
16 Plants
Placed 3 inches apart:
Carrot

Radish

Onion

To help keep up with this, you may want to copy this chart so you always have it handy. Some people even have it laminated so they can take it outdoors without worrying about the weather destroying it.

Another way to get the proper spacing and number per square foot is to be a little more scientific and do a little arithmetic as shown below.

You can see that one, four, nine, or sixteen plants should be spaced an equivalent number of inches apart. This is the same distance the seed packet will say "thin to." Of course we don't have to "thin to" because we don't plant a whole packet of seeds anymore. So if you're planting seeds, or even putting in transplants that you purchased or grew from seed, just find the seed packet or planting directions to see what the distance is for thinning. This distance then determines whether you're going to plant one, four, nine, or sixteen plants.

Just because we're talking about measuring in inches doesn't mean you have to get out your ruler or yardstick, and you don't have to do any complicated measuring or figuring either. This is when the grid becomes handy. When your square foot is bordered by a grid, it's much easier to think one, four, nine, or sixteen plants in each square foot.

All you do is draw lines in the soil with your fingers! For one plant per square foot just poke a hole in the middle of the square with your finger. For four per square foot, draw a vertical and horizontal line dividing the square in half each way. The plants go right in the center of these four smaller squares.

HOW MUCH TO PLANT

I recommend, especially at the beginning, that you plant only what you want to eat. Occasionally try something new, of course, but especially at first only grow those vegetables and herbs that you normally eat.

Remember, plant each adjoining square foot with a different crop. Why? Here are several reasons:

1. It prevents you from overplanting any one particular item.

2. It allows you to stagger your harvest by planting one square foot this week and another of the same crop in two weeks or so.

3. It promotes conservation, companion planting, crop rotation, and allows better plant hygiene and reduced pest problems.

4. It automatically helps to improve your growing soil three times a year in very easy, small steps. Remember the saying, "Square by square, you'll soon be there."

5. Besides all of the above, it looks pretty.

Just like a patchwork quilt, the different colors, leaf textures, plant densities, shapes, and heights, plus the visible grid will give you a very distinctive, photo-opportunity garden. You'll just love and admire it everytime you see it.

Some people ask, "Why can't we plant all sixteen squares with leaf lettuce or spinach or Swiss chard or whatever we want to plant?" Oh, that's going right back to the single-row mentality. Square Foot Gardening begins with visualizing the harvest. It's very difficult to put in four tiny plants of Swiss chard and think that's going to be enough for the whole family, but one square of red and one square of green chard usually is more than most families eat. Proof of the pudding ... how many bunches of Swiss chard did you buy last week or even last month? The stores have it, it's fresh, and it looks good, so why didn't you buy any more than you did? Well, it's the same answer as to why you shouldn't plant too much of one thing.

It's worth repeating here that the biggest problem for single-row gardeners has always been "I planted too much. I can't take care of it. It's too much work and I'm sorry now." All that has changed with SFG and you now have boundaries (the grid) and the opportunity to ask yourself, "For every single square foot I plant, is that enough? Do I really want more? Would it be better to plant another square foot of the same thing in a week or two or three?"

TIME OF YEAR

Keep in mind that you can build a Square Foot Garden anytime of the year—spring, summer, fall, and even winter. For most of the country, you could start planting in any season odier than winter. What time of the year is it right now for you and where are you in the sequence of a yearly gardening cycle? Think of it like the movie theater before the main feature. You're all settled in with your popcorn, ready to devote your full attention to the movie. In the gardening year, this is usually the equivalent of springtime. What if you came in the middle of the picture? For gardening that would be summertime. You can still plant a warm-weather crop even if you missed the spring crop. If it's now fall, you can still start your SFG with a great cool-weather crop and get some valuable experience before next spring. Start whenever you get the urge to plant.

For convenience, we'll start with the beginning of the garden year for most of the country, springtime. (Some parts of the country, like Texas and Florida, can grow all year long. You lucky people.)

Seasonal Plants

You can get at least three crops a year in every square foot of your SFG. Every choice is going to be fun, exciting, and tasty. Of course, your selection depends on the time of year, and what you and your family need and want. There are two types of crops when you consider weather. The first are called cool-weather crops that do best in the spring and fall, but won't survive in the hot summer. The second group is the warm-or hot-weather crops that, you guessed it, don't do well in the cool weather of spring and fall, but thrive in the hot weather of summer.

SEQUENCE OF GROWTH

Did you know that plants grow and bloom everywhere in the same sequence? In other words, throughout the country, daffodils bloom in the springtime, then a little later tulips bloom, then it's time for the lilacs to bloom. (Did I leave out dandelions?) Start noticing the sequence in your location. It would include trees, shrubs, flowers, even weeds.

I read a book once about following spring north. It's theoretically possible that if you drive fast enough (and eat and sleep quickly), you could see nothing but tulips in bloom all the way from Georgia to Maine.

If you know what kinds of plants are summer crops (the most popular and well-known vegetables), it's easy to remember that everything else is a spring or fall crop. Summer crops include beans, peppers, eggplants, tomatoes, and squash. If you plant these when it's too early or cool, they'll either die or their growth will most likely be stunted for that year.

PLAN ON A FALL CROP

As soon as the summer crop is finished, you're ready to plant cool-weather crops for the upcoming fall. These crops are frost-hardy, meaning that both young and mature plants withstand frost. The seeds you plant at the end of summer will sprout quickly since the soil is warmer. Transplants can begin outdoors and grow much faster than the same thing planted in the spring. Look at the charts; compare sprouting times for the same seeds in both spring and summer temperatures.

The fall crop gains an extra advantage from late summer weather. The problem with cool-weather plants in the spring is not cool weather but warm weather at harvest time. A plant's purpose in life is to reproduce seed, and the rising temperatures of an approaching summer make this happen sooner. As it does so, the plant's whole character changes. Many people don't realize that plants like lettuce put up a flower stalk, which then goes to seed. If you wait too long to harvest lettuce, the stalk will shoot up, and the same thing happens to other crops like cabbage. The head splits open, a stalk shoots up, develops flowers, and then turns to seed. It's nature's way of allowing the plant to reproduce, but the plant changes taste when this happens. All the energy goes toward the seed and the plant itself, as far as taste is concerned, becomes rather tough, coarse, and bitter.

In cooler weather, this process is delayed. The plant feels no urgency to complete the growing cycle. So in the fall, the plant slows its maturation process, allowing it to maintain flavor for a longer length of time as temperatures continue to grow cooler and cooler. If it's frost-hardy, it doesn't matter if it is the middle of fall and you start getting frost. Some plants can endure some freezing and still provide a crop for harvesting. Fall is a great time to plant if you put in the right crops.

SOIL TEMPERATURE

Soil temperatures vastly influence sprouting times. For example, if you plant carrot seeds in the summertime when the temperature of the soil is between 60 and 80 degrees Fahrenheit, the seeds will sprout in less than a week. But if you plant the same seeds in early spring when the ground temperature is perhaps 40 degrees, they will take a month and a half to sprout. Just another 10 degrees warmer and they will sprout in a little over two weeks. The chart shows that when the soil is cold and freezing, no seeds will sprout. When it warms up to 40 only half of them will sprout; but as soon as it gets to 50 degrees, suddenly almost all of them will sprout and will continue right through the warmer temperatures of summer and fall.

What happens to seeds when they don't sprout because the ground is cold? They could rot, or fungus could attack them. They could break their dormancy and then go dry. They could be attacked by insects, or dug up by animals or birds. So, the quicker you can get them to sprout the better off they will be.

SPRING, SUMMER, AND FALL CROPS

Some crops, like the cabbage family, take so long to grow that there isn't enough time to plant seeds directly in the garden and wait for the harvest. So you have to buy from nurseries or raise your own transplants indoors ahead of time.

The same situation applies to the warm-weather summer crops like tomatoes, peppers, and eggplants. They take so long to produce that you must plant your garden with transplants. The charts show this all in detail, indicating when to start seeds and when to transplant.

The fall crop is better for raising your own transplants because you will be able to start the seeds in the summertime, raise the transplants outdoors in your garden, and then move them into their permanent spot in the early fall for late fall harvest.

A TYPICAL GARDEN

Let's plant one 4x4 and see how much we will grow in those 16 square feet. We'll start with tall plants on the north side of the box so they don't shade shorter plants. Then put some colorful flowers in each corner. Let's assume it is still springtime, but that we're past the last frost, so we could put four pansies in each corner using our favorite colors.

Carrots require little care until they're harvested. So let's plant two squares of different carrots in the center squares, one square of sixteen onions and a low-maintenance square of sixteen radishes in the center. Then we'll put one square of nine beets in an outside square because we'll harvest their leaves during the season and then finally pull the beet bottoms later. We can plant two or three varieties of leaf lettuce on the outside, depending on your tastes. In another square we could put sixteen chives, and four parsley plants in another, which would provide us a continual harvest. For more color we might want to put a square of red salvia along the back. And perhaps in one corner some dwarf dahlias, one per square foot. Or perhaps some nasturtiums spaced at one per square foot. One of the first things we would have planted in die spring is one or two squares of spinach, nine per square foot. Then depending on your family's taste we could have one or more squares from the cabbage family. That could be red or green cabbage, broccoli, or cauliflower. Keep in mind this is not the only 4 x4 in the whole garden. So we don't have to put all the cabbage into one SFG. It's better to space them out throughout the garden—makes it harder for the cabbage moth to find them all.

PLANS AND DRAWINGS

Remember I mentioned that some people feel a desire to think ahead and draw up a list of everything to be planted in their garden. Then there are even some people who want to assign those plants to spaces ahead of time. So it means drawing a chart, more or less to scale, of your garden and assigning those particular crops to each square foot. Despite being an engineer, who loves charts and diagrams, I don't usually do that. I just like to plant as I see fit. It's very easy to stand in the garden and as the square becomes vacant you just look around and decide it's time to plant another square of radishes. Or maybe you'd like to have some more beans, but this time you'll put in the yellow variety instead of green. It's also very easy to spot and plant where you'd like some color. I find it very easy to just bring home a four-pack of flowers I liked at the nursery and decide by looking at the garden where they would look best. But it's your Square Foot Garden, and you should do whatever makes you happy.

REPLANTING

Keep in mind that, as soon as you harvest, it won't be a big deal to replant because you're going to do it one square foot at a time. Once your newly planted garden starts maturing in the spring—for example, that square foot of radishes will be ready to harvest in four weeks—you'll be ready to replant just that one square. The season has changed and it's warmer, and most of your summer crops can now be planted. So your choices have increased and also most of the summer crop is fairly long-lived and will be in that spot through the whole summer season. As you replant you keep the same criteria in mind—taller plants on the north side to keep them from shading other plants, working your way to cascading flowers on the front corners to look pretty. Place plants that don't need much attention and only occasional harvesting like peppers on the inside, and shorter plants and those that need constant care or harvest to the outside just to make them easier to tend.

WEEDING

This could be the shortest paragraph in the entire book. To start with, your Mel's Mix has no weed seeds in it, and any weeds that do sprout are easily observed because they're not in the proper space and they look different from the plants that are there. Because the soil is so soft and friable weeds come out easily — root and all. You have to weed about once a month. End of paragraph; end of story.

YOU'VE LEARNED THE BASICS

You've now learned all the basics of Square Foot Gardening. You've learned how it got its name—from the squares of one, two, three, four. You have also learned how many and what kind of plants fit into a square foot by memorizing, calculating, or by looking it up on the chart. You've learned how to zip zap in the soil to get the proper and exact spacing then start planting your seeds and transplants. Are we having any fun yet? Next chapter we're going to discuss how to maintain and harvest your SFG.

Okay, now it's time to go out to your garden and do something outrageous that will amaze or dumbfound any neighbor who might be watching you. Do you know how to do a rain dance?

Chapter 4
PLANT AND PROJECTS

MAKING A FORMAL POND

Raised beds don't have to be filled with soil or compost. They can, of course, be filled with water and packed with attractive and colorful aquatic plants.

Raised ponds are useful if you have small children as it is not so easy for them to fall in. They also raise the height of the aquatic life up closer to eye level.

Raised ponds can have seating around the outside, which makes a lovely place to sit and gaze down into the water.

Siting your pond

There is nothing better than a water feature in the garden, whether it is for attracting frogs, newts, and other wildlife or for just lazy days staring at reflections and the light and shade playing on the surface of the water. If formal ponds are placed in direct sunlight they can be prone to a lot of algae, making the water green, so it is a good idea to place one in dappled light. Think about the positioning carefully. Do you want to access all sides of the pond? Do you want to make a central feature or focal point out of it, in which case, you will want to place it in the center of the garden and have paths leading up towards it? Alternatively, you may wish it to be something that you come across as you walk around the garden, in which case you may wish to think of screening or hedging to create a secluded corner somewhere.

How to make a formal pond

Formal ponds imply straight lines and a sense of symmetry to the design. They can be built out of bricks, rocks, or lumber. The project below is made out of railroad ties because it is so simple to build, and the chunky, wide lumber also provides a great place to sit.

Avoid using recycled railway ties as they will leach out creosote and tar in warm weather, which could affect the wildlife in the pond. It will also make a mess of your clothes if you sit on it.

1 | Lay the ties on their edge out on the ground in the shape of a rectangle where you intend to have the raised pond. Make sure that the ground is level using a level tool.

2 | Screw through the corners of the ties to attach them to each other. Screws should go in at least 2 inches into the other board.

3 | If you intend to create more layers of ties then place them on top. Rather than using massive screws to drill through the top of one tie into the one below, it is easier to drill down at 45 degrees through the side of the top railroad tie and into the lower one.

4 | Once you have the right height for the raised pond, use an old carpet to lay across the fl oor and sides of the pond, to prevent sharp edges such as stones puncturing the pond liner.

5 | Place the liner in the bottom of the pond and up the sides.

*To hold the liner in place, attach another railroad tie to create
a top layer and hide the pond liner. There are lots of different
types of pond liners available from garden centers and
specialist aquatic centers, or online. Liners vary in quality
and thickness. At the cheaper end are PVC liners, but the best
ones are rubber based, made from butyl.*

6 | Fill the pond up with water to the height of the liner.

*7 | Add oxygenating plants and other aquatic plants. You can
also introduce fi sh such as koi carp to your pond, should you
want to.*

Aquatic plants for your pond

Oxygenating plants (also called submerged plants) Are
placed under the water. As their name suggests, They release
oxygen, helping to keep the water clean and prevent it from
turning green. Some oxygenators
can become invasive if left to their own devices—you may need
to occasionally lift them out, cut them back by half and replace
the remainder in the water. Popular Plants include:

: *callitriche hermaphroditica* (water starwort)

: *fontinalis antipyretica* (willow moss)

: *hippuris vulgaris* (mare's tail)

: *lobelia dortmanna* (water lobelia)

: *ranunculus aquatilis* (water crowfoot)

Floating plants don't root in the soil but float on the
Surface or just below it, helping to reduce the pond's
Exposure to direct sunlight, which in turn helps to

Reduce the growth of algae. Aim for about 50 percent
Coverage of the surface of the water with plants. Popular
Plants include:

: *azolla mexicana* (mexican water fern)

: *hydrocharis morsus-ranae* (frogbit)

: *stratiotes aloides* (water soldier)

Water lilies are the quintessential pond plant with
Their attractive flower heads and broad leaves that
Float on the surface. They vary in the depth they need
To be planted in the pond, so check with the aquatic
Nursery or plant center before purchasing to ensure it is
Suitable for your pond. Popular plants include:

: *nymphaea alba* (white water lily)

: *n.* 'amabilis'

: *n.* 'gladstoneana'

: *n.* 'gonnère'

: *n.* 'james brydon'

: *n.* 'rose arey'

: *n.* 'william falconer'

: *n.* 'aurora'

: *n. Odorata* var. *Minor*

: *n. Tetragona*

RAISED BED DINING AREA

Raised beds lend themselves very well to the production of food, so to use them to enclose an outdoor dining area seems obvious. The design can incorporate a cooking area, such as a barbecue, clay oven, or firepit, with the plants in the raised beds grown to provide the ingredients. Some ornamental plants included in the plantings will provide a congenial ambience. All green waste should be added to the compost heap.

Materials

The choice of construction materials for a raised bed dining area are very important, and must go beyond the purely functional. Aesthetics are key, and whether you choose a modern design with metal-edged beds, classic stone, or rustic wood is up to you. Functionality, however, must not be overlooked: have you allowed enough room for people to sit and move around? Are there enough surfaces for drinks and condiments? All of this can take up a considerable amount of room, so before you start make sure you allocate ample space.

Plants

In the raised beds themselves you will want to plant a happy mixture of vegetables and herbs so that you have just enough for the kitchen and just enough for show. It is a balance of productivity and ornament, and to achieve this include a few flowering plants, preferably edible ones, amongst the crops. If, through harvesting, you create patches of bare soil in your raised bed, be quick to replant; garden centers are a ready source of filler plants in the summer. Plants can also be used to create screening and shelter. If you are overlooked, or wish to provide shade, build some wire supports into your design so that not only can climbing plants be grown onto them, but also some kind of shade or awning can be attached.

Location

Perhaps the most important factor is to choose a site that is sheltered and intimate. Unless you plan to have a fully functioning kitchen built into the design, it pays for the dining area to be near the house so that you do not have to walk great distances every time you need something from the refrigerator, for example.

ROSES

Roses are quite fussy about the soil they grow in, requiring a heavy, rich soil and fertile ground. Raised beds provide the perfect solution for those people with impoverished soil in their garden. Another benefit is that by growing the roses higher off the ground, it is easier to appreciate their color and scent.

Roses come in all shapes and sizes, from huge rambling and climbing types to low-growing shrubby ones. They come in almost every range of color, except blue, and most of them provide an exquisite floral scent that perfumes the garden. There are thousands of roses to choose from, and new ones are produced each year from plant nurseries. It is generally thought that some of the older shrub roses have the best scent, but this isn't always the case. Visit public parks and gardens with rose gardens and write down the names of the ones that catch your eye. Some roses are prone to diseases such as blackspot and mildew, so it could be worth choosing varieties which have some resistance.

This rose garden is designed for a raised bed measuring 10 feet by 10 feet, but more or fewer plants can be added if you have different size beds. The style of raised bed is up to you, depending on what fits in with your existing garden.

PERMACULTURE RAISED BED

Permaculture, or woodland kitchen gardening, is now increasing in popularity and a mini self-sufficient woodland can be created easily in a moderately sized raised bed.

What is permaculture?

The principles of permaculture rely on using three different tiers or different heights of canopies and plants, which are ground cover, shrubs, and small trees. All three levels provide a variety of habitats for wildlife and help to create a self-sustaining garden, whereby they all benefit from each other. The lower tier helps to suppress weeds while the highest tier provides dappled shade and prevents the woodland floor from drying out. The middle tier provides a link for small mammals and other wildlife between the top and bottom of the garden. Because permaculture is based on natural woodland planting it looks great when planted in a very simplistic, rustic raised bed using lengths of logs or trunks for edging. It's a very rudimentary form of creating a raised bed, but it can look effective when planted up with fruiting shrubs and trees. It is best to use hardwood to create the raised beds, such as oak, beech, or ash as they will last for between five and ten years. Softwood will only last for about three.

HARDY ANNUALS

The cheapest way to grow plants is to sow annuals from seed. For hardly any money at all, literally the price of a few packets of seeds, you can have a fantastic display of bright, colorful flowers.

Annuals couldn't be simpler to grow and once they germinate there is very little maintenance required—just leave them to do their thing, which is flowering their hearts out all summer long.

In this planting design only the sweet peas and sunflowers need to be grown in pots first before planting out. The other plants listed just need to be scattered onto the soil and raked in during spring. It couldn't be easier.

Hardy annuals tend to suit the rustic, cottage garden look, so bear this in mind when deciding what type of raised bed to grow them in. They'll look good in chunky timber or woven willow. Recycled bricks will also add charm to the planting scheme. Most hardy annuals prefer to be grown in full sun in well-drained soil. Add plenty of organic matter to the soil. These annuals need to make all their growth, flower and seeds in one season, so they need as big a boost as they can get once they start germinating.

PLANTING SUGGESTIONS:

: *Lathyrys* (sweet peas)

: *Helianthus* (sunflowers)

: *Centaurea cyanus* (cornflower)

: *Calendula officinalis* (pot marigold)

: *Limnanthes douglasii* (poached egg flower)

: *Lunaria annua* (honesty)

: *Nigella damascena* (love-in-a-mist)

: *Consolida* (larkspur)

: *Papaver commutatum, P. rhoeas, P. somniferum* (corn and opium poppies).

Sunflowers come in a variety of heights, colors, and flower types (single and double). Sow a mixture for a more interesting display.

1 | In the center of the raised bed create a teepee structure using 6 foot bamboo stakes. Space the stakes out equally in a 1 yard-diameter circle.

Lean all the stakes inwards and tie them together with garden twine at the top.

2 | Place two sweet pea seedlings at the base of each stake. Lean the plant toward the structure. This will encourage its tendrils to reach up and attach to the stakes as it starts to grow. The sweet peas can be grown earlier in autumn, by sowing a seed in small pots in general compost and keeping it on a windowsill or in a greenhouse over winter. Plant them out in spring.

3 | The giant sunflowers can be planted toward the back of the raised bed.

Space them 12 inches apart and place a stake next to each one for them to grow up. The sunflowers can be sown in small plastic pots in seedling mix in spring and planted out when they are between 4-8 inches tall. Alternatively, they can be sown directly in the soil where they are to be grown.

4 | With the remainder of the hardy annual seeds use sand to create patterns on the surface of the soil and then sprinkle the packets of seeds into them. Rake them gently into the soil and water using a watering can with a breaker attachment.

5 | It may be necessary to protect newly sown seeds from birds by placing a net over the raised bed until they have germinated.

GOURMET VEGETABLE GARDEN

Carrots: Although carrots are easy to find in the shop, there are some more quirky, unusual varieties that are not often found. The small globe carrots 'Parmex' taste sweet and are great eaten either raw in salads or added to stews and casseroles. There are also purple and yellow carrots worth trying, such as 'Purple Haze' or 'Yellowstone'.

Sow carrots into shallow rows just 1/4 inch deep directly into the soil and water them in well. Thin the seedlings out when they get to about 3 inches tall to leave 3 inches between each plant.

Potatoes: These are cheap to buy and readily available but there are a few varieties that you can't buy for love or money. Try 'Salad Blue', which produce blue potatoes that retain their color after cooking, or 'Burgundy Red' for red ones. Potatoes should be planted in springtime in a trench about 10 inches deep and about 4 inches apart. Backfill with a mix of compost and soil. Potatoes are ready after the plants have flowered. Use a fork to dig them out of the ground. For a small raised bed it is probably only worth growing about five tubers so as not to take up too much space.

Courgettes: Courgettes can be pricey to buy in the shops yet one or two plants will produce bumper crops each year. And choose some of the more interesting colors and flavors such as white, black, or yellow varieties.

Courgettes need to be planted in individual pots from mid to late spring. Place the seed on its side so that it doesn't rot. Plant them out in the raised bed after the risk of frost is over, because they are tender. Add plenty of organic matter to the planting hole prior to planting as they are hungry plants. Keep them well watered and feed them once a week with a liquid fertilizer. A raised bed will only need one or two plants as they should produce bumper crops that will easily be enough to feed a family throughout summer.

Salad leaves: Lettuces can easily be bought from the shops, but there are lots of interesting salad leaves that are easy to grow, such as rocket, mizuna, radicchio, and lots of cut-and-come-again salads, worth trying. Salad leaves can be sown directly into the soil in shallow rows in raised beds. Sow in spring and keep them watered. Most can be cut to near ground level with scissors and they should regrow new leaves, ready for harvesting a few weeks later. Regularly sow every few weeks to ensure there are always plenty of leaves to harvest.

Beans and peas: There are lots of colorful beans and peas, such as 'Purple Teepee' French bean and the purple mangetout 'Shiraz'.

Peas can be sown directly in the soil from early

spring. Plant them about 6 inches apart and push in pea sticks for them to clamber up.

Beans can be sown in pots from mid to late spring. Plant them out after the risk of frost is over. Dwarf varieties can be chosen to make harvesting easier from a raised bed.

Tomatoes: There's a huge range of exciting and colorful tomatoes to try, such as the huge beefsteak variety called 'Black Russian' or the small yellow 'Golden Sweet'.

The best time to sow tomatoes is early spring. Alternatively, buy young plants, as there is an increasing range of unusual types available now as seedlings. Sow them in individual pots indoors and keep them on a windowsill or in a greenhouse until the risk of frost is over. Then plant them out in a sheltered, warm area of the raised bed. They will need supporting with stakes or cages to train them up. Give them a liquid feed with tomato fertilizer once a week once they start to form flowers.

Lightning Source UK Ltd.
Milton Keynes UK
UKHW021257180621
385747UK00002B/346